Romantic Questions

♥ *264 Outrageous, Sweet, and Profound Questions* ♥

Gregory J.P. Godek

SOURCEBOOKS CASABLANCA™
AN IMPRINT OF SOURCEBOOKS, INC.®
NAPERVILLE, ILLINOIS

Published by Sourcebooks, Inc.
P.O. Box 4410, Naperville, Illinois 60567-4410
(630) 961-3900
FAX: (630) 961-2168
www.sourcebooks.com

Previously published as *Intimate Questions*

The Library of Congress has cataloged the previous edition as follows:

Godek, Gregory J.P.
  Intimate Questions: 459 ways to bring you closer/Gregory
Godek.
    p. cm.
  ISBN 1-57071-727-3 (alk. Paper)
  1. Man-woman relationships—Miscellanea. 2. Intimacy
(Psychology)—Miscellania I. Title.
HQ801 .G5546 2001
306.7—dc21

Printed and bound in the United States of America
VP 10 9 8 7 6 5 4 3 2

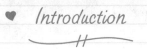

Introduction

A book of questions should begin with questions, don't you think?

Why did you buy this book? What do you hope to discover about yourself? What do you hope to learn about your partner? Are you seeking a method for exploring yourself and your relationship? If so, this book is designed specifically as a tool to help you on your path of discovery.

Questions are powerful. Questions are tools. Questions can be points of leverage. Questions can challenge your assumptions and beliefs. Questions lead to answers!

Some of the questions in this book are deceptively simple. Some are familiar—but deserve revisiting. Some may be shocking. But all of them are designed to help you understand yourself, your partner, and your relationship.

So, why don't we get started?!

♥ *Gregory J.P. Godek*

♥ Partnership ♥

We partner up, two-by-two, automatically. Human beings seem to function better in pairs. This does *not* mean, however, that it's going to be easy!

1.

What are the three best things about your partner?

2.

What made you fall in love with your partner?

3.

What do you and your partner usually argue about?

♥ A Question of Balance ♥

Successful couples are good at balancing their needs, wants, and different personalities.

4.

How do you balance your needs
with your partner's needs?

5.

How do you balance your personal life,
professional life, and social life?

♥ Battle of the Sexes ♥

The last time I checked, men and women weren't at war.
Let's declare "peace" in the Battle of the Sexes, okay?

6.

What is the most mysterious thing about the opposite sex?

7.

What's wrong with men? What's wrong with women?

8.

Do you consider yourself/your attitudes/your
beliefs to be fairly typical for your gender?

9.

If you were going to write a self-help relationship
book, what would you title it?

10.

Are there any circumstances in which it would be appropriate for a man to physically strike a woman?

♥ Beliefs ♥

How your life unfolds is largely the result of the
things you believe. (Do you believe this?)

11.

Do you believe in karma?

12.

Do you believe in an afterlife? In heaven?
In hell? In reincarnation?

13.

Do you believe in astrology? Tarot? Palmistry?

14.

Do you believe in the religion you were raised in?

15.

Do you believe that the Bible is the inspired
word of God? Do you believe it literally—
or do you believe it's open to interpretation?

16.

Do you believe it's proper for people
to express their feelings in public?

♥ Business as Usual ♥

What is your "world view"? How do your views coincide
with and differ from those of your partner?

17.

Do you believe that most people are honest?

18.

Should smoking tobacco be banned?
Should smoking marijuana be legalized?

19.

Should handguns be licensed?
Should toy guns be banned?

♥ Change ♥

You will experience lots of change in any long-term relationship. Don't let it take you by surprise!

20.

Do you change? Or do things change around you?

21.

How have you changed for the better?
How have you changed for the worse?

22.

What was the single most significant
turning point in your life?

23.

What person, book, movie, song, etc.,
has helped you change for the better?

24.

How do you think your life will change most dramatically
in the next five years? Ten years? Twenty years?

♥ Could You...? ♥

Do you know what your capabilities are? It's wise to know your limitations; it's exhilarating to push your limits.

25.
Could you run five miles right now?

26.
Could you survive alone in the wilderness for a week?

27.
Could you kill a person if you had to?

28.
Could you live for a year in a tent with your partner? (Without going crazy?!)

29.
Could you change jobs and move to a different city to be with your mate?

♥ Do You...? ♥

Your beliefs shape your personality. They affect your everyday behavior and how you treat your partner.

30.
Do you vote?

31.
Do you believe in God?

32.

Do you often rethink your decisions, or are
you always certain that you're right?

♥ Do You Agree? ♥

What is your "Philosophy of Life"? One way of
getting a handle on it is to see if you agree or
disagree with the following statements.

33.

Absence makes the heart grow fonder.

34.

Money makes the world go round.

35.

All you need is love.

36.

It is better to give than to receive.

♥ Dreams ♥

Some people have big dreams. Others just dream their
lives away. How do you deal with your dreams?

37.

What is your dream job? What company? What role?
What industry? What product or service?

38.

What is your dream home? Where? Why?

39.

What is your dream vacation?
Where? How long? What activities?

♥ Either, Or ♥

Either, or; this or that; now or then. There's no right or
wrong (or is there?!)—just your opinion. Either way,
your partner deserves to know more about you!

40.

Are you a cat person or a dog person?

41.

Are you outspoken or quiet?

42.

Are you an outdoors person or a homebody?

♥ Erotic ♥

Sure, it can be difficult talking about
intimate issues, but let's give it a try...

43.

What is the difference between sexy and erotic?

44.

What is the most erotic movie scene you've ever seen?

45.

What words do you want to hear during lovemaking?

46.

What are the two most sensitive areas of your body?

47.

What kind of clothing do you find sexy? How would you like your partner to dress during lovemaking?

♥ Fame ♥

This is not the time to be modest. Do you feel comfortable sharing your secret desires with your partner?

48.

If you could accomplish one crazy stunt that would land you in the *Guinness Book of World Records*, what would it be?

49.

If your name were to appear in the dictionary, how would you define yourself?

50.

The editors of *Bartlett's Familiar Quotations* want to include the quote that you're most famous for. What is it?

♥ Family Ties ♥

A great deal of your personality was formed by
your family. So let's take a closer look...

51.

How are you just like your father? Your mother?

52.

Do you like the town you grew up in? Describe it.

53.

What is your fondest memory from childhood?
Worst memory from childhood?

54.

When was the last time you called your mom,
just to tell her you love her? Your dad?

♥ Favorite Things ♥

The better you know your partner, the better you'll
be able to find, buy, or create appropriate gifts.

55.

What is your favorite movie? Actor?
Actress? Comedy? Drama?

56.

What is your favorite dinner? Snack food?
Fancy restaurant? Fast-food restaurant? Dessert?

57.

What is your favorite color?

58.

What is your favorite number?

♥ Would You...? ♥

Would you take the time to answer a few questions
for your lover?

59.

Would you ever go skinny-dipping? With your
partner in private? With a group of other people?

60.

Would you pick up a hitchhiker?

61.

Would you ever run for a political office?

62.

Would you give money to a homeless person?

♥ Feelings ♥

Okay, let's get down to it. Let's try some
creative ways of expressing our feelings.

63.

What movie or TV scene last brought tears to your eyes?

64.

What feeling do you have the most difficulty controlling?
Expressing?

65.

When is the last time you wrote a love letter?

66.

What makes you feel most vulnerable?

67.

When do you feel most fully engaged in living?

68.

What do you do when you feel blue?

69.

What makes you sad? Depressed?

70.

What makes you jealous?

♥ Food, Glorious Food ♥

Is the way to his heart through his stomach?
It's worth a try! (This seems to work equally
well for the women—take note, guys.)

71.

When you sit down in front of a great movie,
what junk food do you want within arm's reach?

72.

You can obliterate one kind of food from
the face of the earth. What food is it?

73.

Are you a picky eater?

♥ For Marrieds Only ♥

To have and to hold, for better or for worse, from this
day forward, I now pronounce you husband and wife.

74.

Before anything was "official," how did you
know you were going to marry each other?

75.

Where were you when you proposed
(or were proposed to)? Exactly what was said?

76.

As you were growing up, what kind of
person did you imagine you'd marry?

77.

What is the funniest/most embarrassing/most touching
thing that happened during your wedding?

78.

Do you believe that you and your spouse
were destined to be together?

♥ For Men Only ♥

Okay, guys, listen up! I know you sometimes
have difficulty expressing your feelings.
But we all know they're in there…

79.

What's the best/worst thing about being male?

80.

Do you feel misunderstood by women?

81.

What is your least masculine attribute?
Are you uncomfortable talking about it?

82.

Which are you more afraid of: cancer or impotence?

83.

Did you ever see your father cry? When?

♥ For Singles Only ♥

Dating shouldn't be about impressing the other person,
but about getting him or her to know you better.

84.

Can you list twenty-five qualities of your perfect partner?

85.

How old do you expect to be when you get married?

86.

Assuming you won't find a partner who is 100 percent perfect, what specific characteristics must your partner possess, and which could you live without?

87.

How important is it that the person you marry share your religious beliefs?

88.

Do you want to have children? How many? Boys or girls? When?

89.

What is the best/worst thing about being single?

90.

What aspect of the single life would you like to carry over into your married life?

♥ For Women Only ♥

Do you think that women are the "fairer sex"? What do you really want men to understand about women?

91.

What is the best/worst thing about being a woman?

92.

Do you experience PMS? How do you want to be treated during your period?

93.

What is your most masculine trait?
Do you use it, or do you tend to suppress it?

94.

Do you feel misunderstood by men?

♥ Getting Down to Business ♥

You'll spend a third to half of your waking hours
at work. What are your attitudes toward work?
How will your work habits affect your relationship?

95.

Do you earn what you're worth?

96.

Do top corporate executives earn too much money?

97.

Should lobbying in Congress be outlawed?

98.

Do doctors earn too much money?
Government workers? Union members? Teachers?

♥ Getting to Know You ♥

Deep down we all want the same thing: to be known,
understood, and appreciated.

99.

Which period of your life did you enjoy the most?
Childhood? Adolescence? Young adulthood?
Adulthood? Right now?

100.

What do you want to be remembered for?

101.

What three famous living people
would you like to be friends with?

♥ Survivor ♥

Some of these "crazy" questions can reveal important
insights into your personality, values, and dreams.
If you were stranded on a desert island...

102.

What three CDs would you most like to have?

103.

Would you wear clothes?

104.

What three books would you want to have with you?

♥ Ha-ha-ha-ha-ha! ♥

People in happy, long-term relationships know that when all else fails, their sense of humor sees them through.

105.

What's your favorite joke?

106.

What's the funniest thing that's ever happened to you?

107.

What's the best practical joke you've ever pulled?

♥ History ♥

Here are some exercises in creative fantasy. Playing the question game of "What if..." can be quite insightful.

108.

If you could become one historical figure, who would it be? Would you change anything about the way he or she lived his or her life?

109.

What are the five greatest achievements of humankind?

110.

If you could have stopped one war from occurring, which one would it be? Why?

111.

You can go back and participate in the writing
of the U.S. Constitution. You can add one
new item to the Bill of Rights. What is it?

♥ Hmmm? ♥

How often do you take time to ponder what
makes you tick? Curiosity about yourself—and
your partner—is a characteristic of lifelong lovers.

112.

Do you believe that marriage is for life?

113.

Which is more important: education or experience?

114.

How often do you talk to your family?

♥ Yikes! ♥

Do you like a good scare? A good surprise?
Do you like roller coasters? Do you like
surprise birthday parties?

115.

What's the luckiest thing that's ever happened to you?

116.
What's the weirdest or creepiest thing
that's ever happened to you?

117.
Who is in charge of the TV remote
control in your relationship?

118.
What activity do you like to do that's "on the edge"?

♥ *If* ♥

This isn't just idle dreaming...it's a door to
your secret dreams and desires. Will you
share them with your partner?

119.
If you could be any age for a day, what age would you be?

120.
If you could change one thing about your parents, what
would it be? How would you be different now if that
change had been made when you were a child?

121.
If you had one million dollars that you had to give away,
who or what would you give it to?

122.

If you could become invisible for a week,
what would you do?

♥ Kid Stuff ♥

A lot of your behavior today is based on your experiences
during the first ten years of your life. How much do you
remember of that time?

123.

What was your favorite toy when you were young?

124.

Did you ever have a nickname?

125.

Did you have a favorite pet when you were a kid?

126.

Who was your "Very Best Friend" at various ages?
What are your best memories of your times together?
Where are they now?

127.

How many brothers and sisters do you have? Do you
think your birth order has affected your personality?

♥ Memories ♥

Do you remember when life was simpler,
less complicated? (Or does it only seem that way?!)

128.

Do you remember your very first kiss?

129.

Who was your first girlfriend or boyfriend?

130.

What did you get away with in high school
that you've still never told anyone about?

131.

What is your earliest memory of childhood?

♥ Miscellaneous ♥

Unusual questions challenge your normal ways of
thinking; they challenge your assumptions.
Therefore, they help to reveal who you really are.

132.

You can create one new national holiday.
What is it called, what does it celebrate,
and on what date does it fall?

133.

What one part of your body would you change?

134.
How many years would you like to live?

135.
What would you like your epitaph to read?

136.
What animal would you like to be?

137.
Who would you like to punch in the nose?

138.
What one bad habit would you like to change?

139.
Who is your best friend in all the world?

140.
God wants an even dozen instead of only Ten Commandments. What are the two new Commandments?

♥ Who Asked You? ♥
One would think that answering questions about one's self would be easy to do. After all, you've lived with yourself all your life! Curious, isn't it?

141.
What book have you been meaning to read?

142.

Where in the world have you always wanted to visit?

143.

If you were a member of the opposite sex,
what would your name be?

♥ Very Interesting ♥

Letting yourself be known—really known—by another
person takes time, understanding, patience, and trust.

144.

Are your "hunches" usually right?
How often do you act on them?

145.

If you were Rick (Humphrey Bogart), in the movie
Casablanca, would you have let Ilsa (Ingrid Bergman) leave
with her husband at the end?

♥ What?! ♥

Do you consider yourself to be creative? Is creativity
a part of your everyday life? Did you know that the
most romantic couples are creatively romantic?

146.

When do you feel most creative?
During what activities are you most creative?

147.

If you had just one more day to live, what would you do?

148.

If you had just six more months to live,
what would you do?

♥ Goals ♥

Do you set goals for yourself? Do you write them down?
How do you celebrate when you accomplish them?

149.

What five accomplishments are you most proud of?

150.

What are your top ten goals for your lifetime?

151.

If you could change one decision you've
made in your life, what would it be?

♥ If You Were King ♥

Have you ever said, "What fools! If only I were
king (queen) of the world, I'd fix things so they'd
work better!" I can't crown you—but I can give
you the opportunity to express your opinions.

152.

Would the world be better off without money?

Taxes? TV? Religion?
The opposite sex? The Pill? Computers?
Rock music? Rap music?
Opera? Football? Cars?
Fundamentalists? Conservatives? Liberals?
Playboy magazine? Nuclear weapons? Welfare?
Cigarettes? Farm subsidies? Congress?
Credit cards? Video games? Handguns?
Lawyers? Talk shows? Speed limits? The Internet?
Advertising? TV weather reporters?
Mandatory schooling? Communism? Capitalism?
Socialism? The *Academy Awards*? Daily newspapers?

♥ Money ♥

Studies show that couples fight about money more
than any other issue. You don't need to see eye-to-eye,
but you'll get along much better if you understand
each other's attitudes about money.

153.

You've just been given one million dollars (tax free).
What is the first thing you'll do tomorrow morning?

154.

You just found a wallet with $500 cash in it. What will
you do with it?

155.

Would you ever spend $300 on a bottle of wine?

♥ More Money ♥

Do you feel better when you have money in the bank? Do you feel good about the way you earn money?

156.

Are you a big spender or a cheapskate?

157.

Should couples have joint or individual bank accounts?

158.

How many credit cards do you have? Why?

159.

What is the single most expensive item you own?

160.

Which would be worse: losing your wallet or being embarrassed in public?

♥ More or Less ♥

Let's face it, we all compare ourselves with others. We can't help it...so let's at least be honest about it!

161.

Are you more or less ambitious than your coworkers?

162.

Are you more or less intelligent than most people?

163.

Are you more or less sensitive than most people?

164.

Are you more or less sensual than most people?

♥ Movie Inspired Questions ♥

Movies have always explored the questions of love. Do you agree with their conclusions? What do you think of the movies' portrayal of love? Of men? Of women?

165.

Can men and women be just friends?
(*When Harry Met Sally*)

166.

Do you need to be accepted by your partner's parents?
(*Meet the Parents*)

167.

Can love last a lifetime? (*The Notebook*)

168.

Is there one perfect person for everyone?
(*Sleepless in Seattle*)

♥ Okay? ♥

Your values are reflected in the kinds of things you approve of and disapprove of. What kinds of issues are you adamant about, and what kinds of issues are you flexible on?

169.

Is it okay for people of different races to date?
To marry? To have children?

170.

Is it okay for your partner to have a
best friend—of the opposite sex?

171.

Is it okay to lie under certain circumstances?
What's the difference between a "little white lie"
and other kinds of lies?

♥ One Day at a Time ♥

Personally, I have a hard time grasping the time frame of a year. It's a lot of time! A month is long, too. Weeks are okay...but a day—one day at a time—is just the right amount of time. I can deal with that. How about you?

172.

What is your favorite time of day?

173.

What are your most and least favorite days of the week?
Why? What could you do to ease the pain?

174.

If you had one extra hour each day, what would you do with it? If there were eight days in a week, what would you do with that extra day?

♥ People ♥

How many people do you like to be around? Many, like at a party? A few, like at an intimate get-together? Just the two of you? Or do you prefer to be alone?

175.

If you could talk with a fictional person, who would it be?

176.

Who are the three greatest people in history?

177.

Who are the people for whom you would do anything?

♥ Perfect ♥

Nobody's perfect—but the idea of what you consider to be perfect/ultimate/awesome tells a lot about you.

178.

What's your idea of the "Perfect Date"?

179.

What's your idea of the "Perfect Kiss"?

180.
What would "Perfect Sex" be like?

♥ Philosophy 101 ♥
You may not think of yourself as a "philosopher,"
but everyone has a "philosophy of life"—a set of
beliefs that guide our actions; a view of life that
explains why things are the way they are.

181.
Why does the world exist?

182.
How did the universe begin?

183.
What one book should everyone in the world
be required to read?

184.
Is there one phrase that sums up your philosophy on life?

♥ Psychological Stuff ♥
Do you know what's going on inside your head?
Do you know what's going on inside your lover's head?
You might want to look into it!

185.
What motivates you to do your best?

186.

What do you feel is your life's central emotional challenge? Intellectual challenge? Career challenge?

187.

What are you afraid of? (Fear of failure? Rejection? Abandonment? Your own anger? Others' anger? Inadequacy?)

188.

Under what circumstance would you seek the help of a counselor or therapist for yourself? Would you consider seeing a couples' counselor if your partner felt it was necessary?

♥ Romance ♥

Do you have enough romance in your life right now? How important is romance in your life?

189.

What is the most romantic thing you've ever done? That's ever been done for you?

190.

Have you ever had a broken heart? How long did it take to heal?

191.

What is the difference between love, romance, and sex?

192.

What is the difference between having sex
and making love?

♥ Say It ♥

We all keep a lot of things inside: feelings, longings,
resentments, desires. Sometimes it's good to express
them. Sometimes simply acknowledging them is enough.

193.

What would you like to say to your father/mother but
just haven't been able to say? Your brothers/sisters?

194.

What do you wish you could say to your boss, but you
don't because you'd probably get fired?

195.

Have you ever said anything that you wish you
could take back? Do you have any regrets?
What is your biggest regret?

♥ School Daze ♥

Did you like school? Were you a member of the "in"
crowd? Did you study much? Did you worry about school?

196.

What was your best/worst subject in grade school?
High school? College?

197.

You can go back and change one thing that happened
to you in high school. What would you change—
and how would this affect your life today?

198.

Do you remember your first school dance? Your favorite
teacher? Your worst experience in gym class?

♥ Secrets ♥

Skeletons in the closet?!—Who me? Not me!
No way! What would make you think such a thing?
(Well, maybe there was this one time...)

199.

Have you ever told something to a stranger on
a plane that you haven't told your partner?

200.

Have you ever cheated in school?
On your taxes? On a significant other?

201.

What if you had to tell the absolute truth
for one solid week?

♥ Intimate Fantasies ♥

Kids know how to fantasize without being
taught. We adults have to relearn how to
let our imaginations run wild again.

202.

What is your secret sexual fantasy? (You know,
that one that you've never shared with anyone.)

203.

Where would you like to have sex? Outside?
Elevator? Living room? Laundry room?
Kitchen table? Back seat of a car?

204.

Ideally, how often would you like to have sex?

♥ Foreplay ♥

Here's where we're really going to uncover some
assumptions between the two of you. Hang in there!

205.

Do you know what your partner's favorite
foreplay activity is?

206.

What is your favorite foreplay activity?
To give? To receive?

207.

Can you describe an orgasm? (What color is it?
Does it tingle, explode, flow? Does it linger?
How long? How else would you describe it?)

♥ Sex ♥

As a culture, we are obsessed with sex.
And yet we rarely really talk about it.

208.

Would you rather be rich or sexy?

209.

What sexual activity have you never done
before but would like to try?

♥ Hot Stuff! ♥

What are your personal turn-ons? You don't have to tell
all of us—just your very own intimate partner.

210.

What are your favorite erotic and/or sexy movies?

211.

Would you like your lover to be more sexually assertive?
How—specifically?

212.

What songs make you think of making love?
Do you own them?

213.

How did you first learn about sex?
What crazy misconceptions did you once have?

♥ Simply Outrageous! ♥

There is a time and a place for acting mature and
grown-up. But it's not always and everywhere! What is
the most wild/outrageous part of your personality?

214.

You can commit one crime and get away with
it completely. What would that crime be?

215.

If you could be a superhero, who would you be?

216.

If you were going to get a tattoo, what would it be?
Where on your body would it be?

♥ Smarty Pants! ♥

There are many ways of being "smart"—just as
there are many ways of being romantic.

217.

Would you rather be really, really smart,
or really, really good looking?

218.

If you had an IQ of 190, how would it change your life?

♥ Supercalifragilisticexpialidocious ♥

Does everything have to make sense?
How imaginative are you?

219.

What are the three greatest inventions of all time?

220.

Would you rather have the power to become
invisible or the power to levitate things?

221.

If you could have great talent in one area, which would
you choose: writing, art, or music? Why?

♥ *Time* ♥

Think about it: Time is your most precious resource
of all. Do you use it wisely? How much of it do
you spend on your relationship?

222.

How much time do you spend thinking about the past?
The future?

223.

How much time do you and your partner spend
together purely having fun (apart from sex)?

224.

How many minutes of undivided attention
per day do you give your partner?

♥ *Togetherness* ♥

It seems to be human nature to want to "couple-up."
Maybe it's true that two heads are better than one!

225.

Can a person be too much in love?

226.

Can you read your partner's mind?

227.

What is the best relationship advice you've ever gotten?

♥ Potpourri ♥

Your thoughts, opinions, and unique points-of-view
make you who you are. Who are you?

228.
Do you have a guardian angel?

229.
Are you happy with your name?
If you could, what would you change it to?

230.
Do you fold your underwear or just stuff it in the drawer?

♥ TV ♥

It's said that the average American watches seven
hours of TV per day! Do you spend as much
time with your partner as with the TV?

231.
Barbara Walters is going to interview you for TV.
What are her first three questions to you?

232.
Is there too much violence on TV? Too much sex?

233.
What TV show are you embarrassed to admit that you enjoy?

♥ You! ♥

Let's get personal. These questions tap into some private parts of your personality. Are you willing to share them?

234.
Would you rather be rich or famous?

235.
If you could save just one object from your burning home, what would it be?

236.
What is your very best quality?
(This is not the time to be modest.)

237.
If you had to be either blind or deaf, which would you choose?

238.
Who do you need to forgive?

♥ You Two ♥

This is about you. And about your partner, too. The two of you. The more you know about each other, the deeper your love can grow.

239.
What makes you nostalgic? Homesick? Thoughtful?

240.

What gives you the creeps?

241.

What makes you horny?

242.

How is your relationship the same as your parents'?
How is it different?

243.

If your partner had an affair, could you
forgive him or her?

♥ Miscellany ♥

There are many, many facets to your personality.
Worth a lifetime of inquiry.

244.

What did you want to be when you grew up?

245.

If men instead of women had babies,
how would the world be different?

246.

Right this minute—as you are reading this—how is your
health? Are you in love? What emotions are you feeling? Do
you wish you were doing something else? Do you feel happy?

♥ Opposites ♥

Opposites attract, right? Sometimes yes, sometimes no.

247.

What was the biggest fight you've ever had
with any member of the opposite sex?

248.

When you were growing up, what was your relationship
like with your parent of the opposite sex?

249.

Which of your character traits is the most
at odds with general cultural norms?

♥ Generations ♥

Your early years have had a vast impact on
who you are today. Family, relatives, and
close friends all leave their mark on you.

250.

Who is your favorite relative? Least favorite? Why?

251.

What life lesson did you learn from one
of your grandparents?

252.

What one wish do you have for your children?

253.

What is your philosophy on raising children?

♥ Dream On ♥

Dreams are a mysterious phenomenon of our existence.
Every belief about them is just a theory. What do you think?

254.

Do you believe that dreams reveal your inner desires?
Are dreams a doorway to your unconscious mind?

255.

Do you believe that dreams can foretell the future?

256.

Do you remember any dreams from your childhood?

♥ Fun, Fun, Fun! ♥

While most of us don't really believe that our
purpose on Earth is to have fun, it certainly
makes being here more worthwhile.

257.

What's the most fun you've ever had with your clothes on?
With your clothes off?

258.

At what age did you start really being
interested in the opposite sex?

259.

Do you play enough now?

♥ Think about It ♥

Here are some things that, perhaps, you've never thought about. Lucky you—now you have the opportunity!

260.

If you went bald, would you wear a toupee/wig?

261.

Would you ever go to a nude beach?

262.

If you were going to appear on David Letterman's "Stupid Human Tricks" segment, what would you do?

♥ Grades ♥

We get graded in school, but from that point forward we rarely use an objective grading system to evaluate ourselves. It might help!

263.

What grade would you give your relationship? (Grade yourself as if in school—A through F.)

264.

What grade would you give your performance at work?

About the Author

Gregory J.P Godek is the author of the bestselling *1001 Ways to Be Romantic* and *10,000 Ways to Say I Love You*. He has written more than a dozen books on being romantic, with more than two million books sold. He lives in La Jolla, California.

Also by Gregory J.P. Godek:

1001 Ways To Be Romantic—
5th Anniversary Edition of the Bestselling Classic!
10,000 Ways to Say I Love You
Enchanted Evenings
LoveQuotes Coupons
I Love You Coupons
Love Coupons
Confessions of a True Romantic
Love—The Course They Forgot to Teach You in School

To order these books or any other of our many publications, please contact your local bookseller, gift store, or call Sourcebooks. Books by Gregory J.P. Godek are available in book and gift stores across North America. Get a copy of our catalog by writing or faxing:

Sourcebooks, Inc
P. O. Box 4410
Naperville, IL 60567-4410
(630) 961-3900
FAX: (630) 961-2168